THE JPS B'NAI MITZVAH TORAH COMMENTARY

Koraḥ (Numbers 16:1–18:32)
Haftarah (1 Samuel 11:14–12:22)

Rabbi Jeffrey K. Salkin

The Jewish Publication Society · Philadelphia
University of Nebraska Press · Lincoln

INTRODUCTION

News flash: the most important thing about becoming bar or bat mitzvah isn't the party. Nor is it the presents. Nor even being able to celebrate with your family and friends—as wonderful as those things are. Nor is it even standing before the congregation and reading the prayers of the liturgy—as important as that is.

No, the most important thing about becoming bar or bat mitzvah is sharing Torah with the congregation. And why is that? Because of all Jewish skills, that is the most important one.

Here is what is true about rites of passage: you can tell what a culture values by the tasks it asks its young people to perform on their way to maturity. In American culture, you become responsible for driving, responsible for voting, and yes, responsible for drinking responsibly.

In some cultures, the rite of passage toward maturity includes some kind of trial, or a test of strength. Sometimes, it is a kind of "outward bound" camping adventure. Among the Maasai tribe in Africa, it is traditional for a young person to hunt and kill a lion. In some Hispanic cultures, fifteen year-old girls celebrate the *quinceañera*, which marks their entrance into maturity.

What is Judaism's way of marking maturity? It combines both of these rites of passage: *responsibility* and *test*. You show that you are on your way to becoming a *responsible* Jewish adult through a public *test* of strength and knowledge—reading or chanting Torah, and then teaching it to the congregation.

This is the most important Jewish ritual mitzvah (commandment), and that is how you demonstrate that you are, truly, bar or bat mitzvah—old enough to be responsible for the mitzvot.

What Is Torah?

So, what exactly is the Torah? You probably know this already, but let's review.

The Torah (teaching) consists of "the five books of Moses," sometimes also called the *chumash* (from the Hebrew word *chameish*, which means "five"), or, sometimes, the Greek word Pentateuch (which means "the five teachings").

Here are the five books of the Torah, with their common names and their Hebrew names.

> Genesis (The beginning), which in Hebrew is Bere'shit (from the first words—"When God began to create"). Bere'shit spans the years from Creation to Joseph's death in Egypt. Many of the Bible's best stories are in Genesis: the creation story itself; Adam and Eve in the Garden of Eden; Cain and Abel; Noah and the Flood; and the tales of the Patriarchs and Matriarchs, Abraham, Isaac, Jacob, Sarah, Rebekah, Rachel, and Leah. It also includes one of the greatest pieces of world literature, the story of Joseph, which is actually the oldest complete novel in history, comprising more than one-quarter of all Genesis.

> Exodus (Getting out), which in Hebrew is Shemot (These are the names). Exodus begins with the story of the Israelite slavery in Egypt. It then moves to the rise of Moses as a leader, and the Israelites' liberation from slavery. After the Israelites leave Egypt, they experience the miracle of the parting of the Sea of Reeds (or "Red Sea"); the giving of the Ten Commandments at Mount Sinai; the idolatry of the Golden Calf; and the design and construction of the Tabernacle and of the ark for the original tablets of the law, which our ancestors carried with them in the desert. Exodus also includes various ethical and civil laws, such as "You shall not wrong a stranger or oppress him, for you were strangers in the land of Egypt" (22:20).

> Leviticus (about the Levites), or, in Hebrew, Va-yikra' (And God called). It goes into great detail about the kinds of sacrifices that the ancient Israelites brought as offerings; the laws of ritual purity; the animals that were permitted and forbidden for eating (the beginnings of the tradition of kashrut, the Jewish dietary laws); the diagnosis of various skin diseases; the ethical laws of holiness; the ritual calendar of the Jewish year; and various agricultural laws concerning the treatment of the Land of Israel. Leviticus is basically the manual of ancient Judaism.

➤ Numbers (because the book begins with the census of the Israelites), or, in Hebrew, Be-midbar (In the wilderness). The book describes the forty years of wandering in the wilderness and the various rebellions against Moses. The constant theme: "Egypt wasn't so bad. Maybe we should go back." The greatest rebellion against Moses was the negative reports of the spies about the Land of Israel, which discouraged the Israelites from wanting to move forward into the land. For that reason, the "wilderness generation" must die off before a new generation can come into maturity and finish the journey.

➤ Deuteronomy (The repetition of the laws of the Torah), or, in Hebrew, Devarim (The words). The final book of the Torah is, essentially, Moses's farewell address to the Israelites as they prepare to enter the Land of Israel. Here we find various laws that had been previously taught, though sometimes with different wording. Much of Deuteronomy contains laws that will be important to the Israelites as they enter the Land of Israel—laws concerning the establishment of a monarchy and the ethics of warfare. Perhaps the most famous passage from Deuteronomy contains the *Shema*, the declaration of God's unity and uniqueness, and the *Ve-ahavta*, which follows it. Deuteronomy ends with the death of Moses on Mount Nebo as he looks across the Jordan Valley into the land that he will not enter.

Jews read the Torah in sequence—starting with Bere'shit right after Simchat Torah in the autumn, and then finishing Devarim on the following Simchat Torah. Each Torah portion is called a parashah (division; sometimes called a *sidrah*, a place in the order of the Torah reading). The stories go around in a full circle, reminding us that we can always gain more insights and more wisdom from the Torah. This means that if you don't "get" the meaning this year, don't worry—it will come around again.

And What Else? The Haftarah

We read or chant the Torah from the Torah scroll—the most sacred thing that a Jewish community has in its possession. The Torah is written without vowels, and the ability to read it and chant it is part of the challenge and the test.

But there is more to the synagogue reading. Every Torah reading has an accompanying haftarah reading. Haftarah means "conclusion," because there was once a time when the service actually ended with that reading. Some scholars believe that the reading of the haftarah originated at a time when non-Jewish authorities outlawed the reading of the Torah, and the Jews read the haftarah sections instead. In fact, in some synagogues, young people who become bar or bat mitzvah read very little Torah and instead read the entire haftarah portion.

The haftarah portion comes from the Nevi'im, the prophetic books, which are the second part of the Jewish Bible. It is either read or chanted from a Hebrew Bible, or maybe from a booklet or a photocopy.

The ancient sages chose the haftarah passages because their themes reminded them of the words or stories in the Torah text. Sometimes, they chose *haftarah* with special themes in honor of a festival or an upcoming festival.

Not all books in the prophetic section of the Hebrew Bible consist of prophecy. Several are historical. For example:

The book of Joshua tells the story of the conquest and settlement of Israel.

The book of Judges speaks of the period of early tribal rulers who would rise to power, usually for the purpose of uniting the tribes in war against their enemies. Some of these leaders are famous: Deborah, the great prophetess and military leader, and Samson, the biblical strong man.

The books of Samuel start with Samuel, the last judge, and then move to the creation of the Israelite monarchy under Saul and David (approximately 1000 BCE).

The books of Kings tell of the death of King David, the rise of King Solomon, and how the Israelite kingdom split into the Northern Kingdom of Israel and the Southern Kingdom of Judah (approximately 900 BCE).

And then there are the books of the prophets, those spokesmen for God whose words fired the Jewish conscience. Their names are immortal: Isaiah, Jeremiah, Ezekiel, Amos, Hosea, among others.

Someone once said: "There is no evidence of a biblical prophet ever being invited back a second time for dinner." Why? Because the prophets were tough. They had no patience for injustice, apathy, or hypocrisy. No one escaped their criticisms. Here's what they taught:

> God commands the Jews to behave decently toward one another. In fact, God cares more about basic ethics and decency than about ritual behavior.
> God chose the Jews *not* for special privileges, but for special duties to humanity.
> As bad as the Jews sometimes were, there was always the possibility that they would improve their behavior.
> As bad as things might be now, it will not always be that way. Someday, there will be universal justice and peace. Human history is moving forward toward an ultimate conclusion that some call the Messianic Age: a time of universal peace and prosperity for the Jewish people and for all the people of the world.

Your Mission—To Teach Torah to the Congregation

On the day when you become bar or bat mitzvah, you will be reading, or chanting, Torah—in Hebrew. You will be reading, or chanting, the haftarah—in Hebrew. That is the major skill that publicly marks the becoming of bar or bat mitzvah. But, perhaps even more important than that, you need to be able to teach something about the Torah portion, and perhaps the haftarah as well.

And that is where this book comes in. It will be a very valuable resource for you, and your family, in the b'nai mitzvah process. Here is what you will find in it:

> A brief **summary** of every Torah portion. This is a basic overview of the portion; and, while it might not refer to everything in the Torah portion, it will explain its most important aspects.
> A list of the **major ideas** in the Torah portion. The purpose: to make the Torah portion real, in ways that we can relate to. Every Torah portion contains unique ideas, and when you put all

of those ideas together, you actually come up with a list of Judaism's most important ideas.

> Two ***divrei Torah*** ("words of Torah," or "sermonettes") for each portion. These *divrei Torah* explain significant aspects of the Torah portion in accessible, reader-friendly language. Each *devar Torah* contains references to **traditional** Jewish sources (those that were written before the modern era), as well as **modern** sources and quotes. We have searched, far and wide, to find sources that are unusual, interesting, and not just the "same old stuff" that many people already know about the Torah portion. Why did we include these minisermons in the volume? Not because we want you to simply copy those sermons and pass them off as your own (that would be cheating), though you are free to quote from them. We included them so that you can see what is possible—how you can try to make meaning for yourself out of the words of Torah.

> **Connections:** This is perhaps the most valuable part. It's a list of questions that you can ask yourself, or that others might help you think about—any of which can lead to the creation of your *devar Torah.*

Note: you don't have to like everything that's in a particular Torah portion. Some aren't that loveable. Some are hard to understand; some are about religious practices that people today might find confusing, and even offensive; some contain ideas that we might find totally outmoded.

But this doesn't have to get in the way. After all, most kids spend a lot of time thinking about stories that contain ideas that modern people would find totally bizarre. Any good medieval fantasy story falls into that category.

And we also believe that, if you spend just a little bit of time with those texts, you can begin to understand what the author was trying to say.

This volume goes one step further. Sometimes, the haftarah comes off as a second thought, and no one really thinks about it. We have tried to solve that problem by including a **summary** of each haftarah, and then a mini-sermon on the haftarah. This will help you learn how these sacred words are relevant to today's world, and even to your own life.

All Bible quotations come from the NJPS translation, which is found in the many different editions of the JPS TANAKH; in the Conservative movement's *Etz Hayim: Torah and Commentary;* in the Reform movement's *Torah: A Modern Commentary;* and in other Bible commentaries and study guides.

How Do I Write a *Devar Torah?*

It really is easier than it looks.

There are many ways of thinking about the *devar Torah.* It is, of course, a short sermon on the meaning of the Torah (and, perhaps, the haftarah) portion. It might even be helpful to think of the *devar Torah* as a "book report" on the portion itself.

The most important thing you can know about this sacred task is: *Learn* the words. *Love* the words. Teach people what it could mean to *live* the words.

Here's a basic outline for a *devar Torah:*

"My Torah portion is (name of portion)_____,
     from the book of _____ , chapter

     _____.

"In my Torah portion, we learn that_____
     (Summary of portion)

"For me, the most important lesson of this Torah portion is (what is the best thing in the portion? Take the portion as a whole; your *devar Torah* does not have to be only, or specifically, on the verses that you are reading).

"As I learned my Torah portion, I found myself wondering:

> *Raise a question that the Torah portion itself raises.*
> *"Pick a fight"* with the portion. Argue with it.
> *Answer a question* that is listed in the "Connections" section of each Torah portion.
> *Suggest a question to your rabbi* that you would want the rabbi to answer in his or her own *devar Torah* or sermon.

"I have lived the values of the Torah by _____
(here, you can talk about how the Torah portion relates to your
own life. If you have done a mitzvah project, you can talk about
that here).

How To Keep It from Being Boring
(and You from Being Bored)

Some people just don't like giving traditional speeches. From our per-
spective, that's really okay. Perhaps you can teach Torah in a different
way—one that makes sense to you.

> Write an "open letter" to one of the characters in your Torah por-
  tion. "Dear Abraham: I hope that your trip to Canaan was not too
  hard . . ." "Dear Moses: Were you afraid when you got the Ten
  Commandments on Mount Sinai? I sure would have been . . ."
> Write a news story about what happens. Imagine yourself to
  be a television or news reporter. "Residents of neighboring cities were horrified yesterday as the wicked cities of Sodom and
  Gomorrah were burned to the ground. Some say that God was
  responsible . . ."
> Write an imaginary interview with a character in your Torah portion.
> Tell the story from the point of view of another character, or a mi-
  nor character, in the story. For instance, tell the story of the Gar-
  den of Eden from the point of view of the serpent. Or the story
  of the Binding of Isaac from the point of view of the ram, which
  was substituted for Isaac as a sacrifice. Or perhaps the story of
  the sale of Joseph from the point of view of his coat, which was
  stripped off him and dipped in a goat's blood.
> Write a poem about your Torah portion.
> Write a song about your Torah portion.
> Write a play about your Torah portion, and have some friends act
  it out with you.
> Create a piece of artwork about your Torah portion.

The bottom line is: Make this a joyful experience. Yes—it could
even be fun.

The Very Last Thing You Need to Know at This Point

The Torah scroll is written without vowels. Why? Don't *sofrim* (Torah scribes) know the vowels?

Of course they do.

So, why do they leave the vowels out?

One reason is that the Torah came into existence at a time when sages were still arguing about the proper vowels, and the proper pronunciation.

But here is another reason: The Torah text, as we have it today, and as it sits in the scroll, is actually *an unfinished work*. Think of it: the words are just sitting there. Because they have no vowels, it is as if they have no voice.

When we read the Torah publicly, we give voice to the ancient words. And when we find meaning in those ancient words, and we talk about those meanings, those words jump to life. They enter our lives. They make our world deeper and better.

Mazal tov to you, and your family. This is your journey toward Jewish maturity. Love it.

THE TORAH

❖ Koraḥ: Numbers 16:1–18:32

In a book that is filled with stories of rebellion against Moses, the greatest rebellion was the one that Korah orchestrated. Korah, a Levite (like Moses and Aaron), insists that the entire Israelite community is holy, and that Moses and Aaron have no right to their positions of authority. God punishes the rebels by having an earthquake swallow them alive.

Perhaps as a way of emphasizing the destructiveness of Korah's behavior, God reemphasizes the sacred duties of the Levites.

Summary

> Korah, along with Dathan and Abiram, starts a revolt against Moses and Aaron. He declares that all the Israelites, and not just Moses and Aaron, are holy. Moses counters Korah by reminding him that, as Levites, he and his buddies already have sacred duties. Moses insists on his innocence and on his righteous behavior, and tells the rebels to bring incense offerings in fire pans. But Korah and his band are not convinced, and the whole incident ends badly, with the group being swallowed up by the earth. (16:1–35)

> The rebels' fire pans become holy and are hammered into the altar. This is to serve as a warning for those who would rebel in the future. (17:1–7)

> God wants to destroy the Israelites, but Aaron puts incense on a fire pan as a way of warding off the plague that would have killed them. (17:8–15)

> As a way of demonstrating the ongoing sanctity of Aaron and the entire tribe of Levi, God instructs Moses to tell the people to take a staff from each tribe, as well as one from the Levites, and place the staffs inside the ark. The staff of the tribe that is to be chosen by God will sprout. And the one that sprouts turns out to be the staff of Aaron. (17:17–28)

The Big Ideas

> For Jews, holiness is not a given; you have to work toward it. In the Holiness Code in Leviticus, God says to Moses: "Speak to the whole Israelite community and say to them: 'You shall be holy' (Lev. 19:1)," But that's a big "shall." The Israelites are not yet holy. That was Korah's fundamental problem: he believed that the "shall" was an "already is," that everyone was already holy and that everyone was equal. It is important to have goals, but be careful not to believe something is so just because you want it to be so. Have goals and work on a way to reach those goals.

> Even rebellion can become holy. This seems odd. The text tells us that the fire pans are hammered into the altar as a warning. But in another sense, perhaps they are also part of the altar as a way of saying that rebellion and questioning will become a constant (and, often, necessary) theme in Jewish life. There are even psalms in the Bible that are said to have been written by "the sons of Korah." And so we see that the prayerful contributions of a rebel's descendants are part of Jewish sacred literature.

> Spiritual heroism entails speaking out and acting in favor of your people. This is the true greatness of Moses (and in this particular instance, Aaron)—the willingness to go to bat for the People of Israel. There were many times when God threatened to destroy the Israelites. But Moses, following the example of Abraham at Sodom and Gomorrah, stands up for his people and convinces God to relent.

> The task of holiness means ongoing growth and renewal. There are few things as lifeless as a plain wooden staff, and few things as miraculous as its ability to sprout into a living organism. That is a good way to think about life, and about Judaism itself— renewable spiritual energy.

Divrei Torah

SOMEONE HAS AN ATTITUDE PROBLEM

A kid in religious school walks in wearing a T-shirt that bears the following words: "I LOVE my attitude problem."

That kid could have been Korah. He had an attitude problem.

Korah gathers together a loose confederation of malcontents and launches a rebellion against the authority of Moses. "You have gone too far! For all the community are holy, all of them, and the Lord is in their midst," he challenges Moses. "Why then do you raise yourselves above the Lord's congregation?" (16:3)

Did Korah have a point? Wasn't he trying to be democratic and egalitarian? What was so bad about what he said that led to such a severe punishment? The sages say that it was his attitude, his motive, that was really at fault. They go so far as to claim that Korah (who was a cousin of Moses and Aaron, by the way) was not so much interested in his own argument as he was in grabbing power from his own relatives.

Let's follow part of the ancient argument. The sages imagine Korah asking Moses: "Does a house that is filled with Torah scrolls require a mezuzah on its door? Does a garment that is entirely blue still need to have a blue thread in its fringes?" The questions make sense on one level. After all, the Torah scrolls contain the entire Torah; the mezuzah contains just a brief passage from Deuteronomy. Shouldn't all those Torah scrolls fulfill the mitzvah of having a mezuzah? And an entirely blue garment should be blue enough without the blue thread, right? And yet, Moses responds by saying that yes, even a house that is filled with Torah scrolls requires a mezuzah, and, yes, even an entirely blue garment needs a blue thread in the tzitzit. Korah goes ballistic and accuses Moses of making the whole thing up just to keep power.

Was Korah right? Well, yes and no. Yes, the sages, in their portrayal of Korah, want Judaism to make sense and to be logical. Korah would have agreed with the twentieth-century writer Edmond Fleg, who said: "I am a Jew because Judaism requires no abdication of the mind." And it is certainly logical that a house filled with Torah scrolls should need no mezuzah, and that a garment that is entirely blue should not need a blue thread in its ritual fringes. We get this. But here is where Korah got it wrong: Jewish practices are not entirely logical. In some ways, Judaism is like an elaborate, ancient game, with its own rules. Many things in many cultures have no logic to them. Dressing up on Halloween—how does that make sense? And what about lighting candles on a birthday cake? We have many customs and rituals that help keep the community together though they are not what we would call *rational*.

So, what was up with Korah? Why did he ask, as the Rabbis imagined, whether a blue garment needs a blue thread in the fringes? Korah thinks that all the Jews are already holy. If all the Jews are already holy, then an all-blue garment should be holy as well. That was his logic.

And the deal about the mezuzah and the Torah scrolls? Here is what Korah did not understand. It's not enough to have Torah scrolls on the inside of your house. No—the mezuzah sits on the doorpost, at the precise intersection of the private and the public, at the place where our inner life ends and our outer life begins. It is there to remind us that when we leave the house, we must take Torah out into the world.

Korah made the mistake, in the eyes of the Rabbis, of assuming that people are already holy, when in reality they must strive to be holy. He made the mistake of thinking that everything must be rational, when some things must be taken on faith. But lurking behind this was the most problematic thing of all: Korah may have hid behind his arguments because he wanted to create a rebellion and seize power for himself.

Now that is an attitude problem!

AARON'S MAGICAL STAFF—A MIRACLE!

There was a time when kids liked to learn magic tricks—mostly card tricks, though some got into more advanced stuff.

There's magic—and, then, there's *real* magic, like a magic staff.

Each of the twelve leaders of the ancestral tribes was asked to inscribe his name on a staff, which was then placed in the Holy Ark in the Tent of Meeting, the Tabernacle (*mishkan*). The next day "the staff of Aaron of the house of Levi had sprouted: it had brought forth sprouts, produced blossoms, and borne almonds" (17:23). This sign reassured the people that Aaron was the true representative of God.

Aaron's staff has an interesting history. The ancient Rabbis imagined that it was part of the very act of creation itself, created in the twilight between the sixth day and the Sabbath. The first time it was used was by Jacob, when he crossed the Jordan River. A midrash says: "That same staff was held in the hand of every king until the Temple was destroyed, and then it was divinely hidden away. That same staff also is destined to be held in the hand of the Messiah."

We are talking about a miraculous staff here. First, for it to blossom is a miracle.

Not only that. After a normal fruit (or nut) tree blossoms, its flowers wither and become buds, which then grow and eventually become fruit (or nuts). But Aaron's staff went through all those stages *at the same time:* "it brought forth sprouts, produced blossoms, and bore almonds" (17:23). In some ways, it is like Judaism today. When the Holocaust occurred, there were people who thought that Judaism was a dry, dead stick—like Aaron's staff before it sprouted. But now many can see that the hard, dry stick has, in fact, blossomed. Think of the modern State of Israel—what a miracle that is. Consider that there is more serious Jewish learning going on today, more Jewish culture than ever before, more Jews serving in important government positions, even Jews who have sought the American presidency. In many respects, Judaism and the worldwide Jewish community is sprouting anew and bearing fruit.

Often in life we become like Aaron's staff. Sometimes we feel dead and wooden. And then things change. We learn new skills, make new friends, and we have new adventures. We go through all stages of growth: flowers, buds, and fruit. We feel hopeful again.

Ah, but why does Aaron's staff bring forth, of all things, almonds? Almonds are both bitter and sweet—sort of like life.

Rabbi Israel Salanter once said: "We live by miracles every day, but miracles don't happen every day." There are miracles in our lives and in our shared history—some we recognize and some we don't. To pass through difficult times, to have hope, and to flourish again—this is truly holy and truly a miracle.

Connections

> Have you ever been part of a rebellion—at home, in school, on a team, in camp, or in religious school? What was it like? What did you learn from that experience?

> Do you think that Korah was right or wrong to rebel against the authority of Moses?

> Were the challenges that Korah posed to Moses in the midrash about the mezuzah and the fringes effective? Why or why not?

> What are some things in Judaism that make sense to you? Some that don't?

> Why do you think this story of rebellion was included in the Torah?

> How would you define a miracle? Have you experienced any in your life?

THE HAFTARAH

❖ Koraḥ: 1 Samuel 11:14–12:22

Some people have trouble with authority. Korah, who is the star of the Torah portion, was one of those people. Korah, a Levite (and cousin to Moses and Aaron), insists that the entire Israelite community is holy, and that Moses and Aaron have no right to their positions of authority. Moses retorts, somewhat defensively: "I have not taken the ass of any one of them, nor have I wronged any one of them" (Num. 16:15).

The ancient Rabbis, who chose the *haftarah* for each Torah portion, took the theme of Korah's rebellion, and they associated it with something that happened centuries later, told in this week's haftarah. The People of Israel gang up on the prophet Samuel and demand that he appoint them a king to rule over them. Samuel responds, in much the same way as Moses did: "Whose ox have I taken, or whose ass have I taken?" (12:3).

The link between the Torah portion and the haftarah is clear: both Moses and Samuel, faced with what seemed to be a rebellion, defend themselves, saying that they have behaved justly. Their example is one that all leaders should imitate.

Give Us a King!

Samuel, like Moses, must have had it up to here with the People of Israel. All they seem to do is nag! And what are they nagging about? They want a king, just like all the other nations. (It's like a mother getting fed up with a kid who is constantly bugging her about something that he wants—just because the other kids have it.)

Samuel was not only a prophet; he was also a judge—a chieftain who ruled the People of Israel. He was an excellent leader, but his sons were not. In fact, you might actually say that they were total screwups. The people become fed up with Samuel's sons. That, too, contributed to their demand for change, and in 1 Sam. 8:6, they ask for a king.

This upsets Samuel, but God tells him that it's not as if the people were rejecting him (Samuel); rather, they were really rejecting God, who should be their true king. Samuel then reads the people the riot act. He warns them of all the possible abuses of power that a king might engage in: a king would draft their sons into his army; he would force them to plow his fields and make his weapons; he would take their land; he would make the women perfumers and cooks (8:10–18). These warnings were very much in line with the passage in Deuteronomy 17, which specifies what kings can and cannot do. That chapter is sometimes called "the chapter of the king," and as the Talmud says: "All that is set out in the chapter of the king, the king is permitted to do."

But the people still insist, so Samuel relents and appoints a king: "I have yielded to you in all you have asked of me and have set a king over you" (12:1).

We really cannot blame the people for wanting a king. After all, Samuel's sons have done a terrible job at leadership. More than this: the people realized that the best way for them to be able to defend themselves against their enemies was to have a king.

More than that: in the "old system," every so often, a judge or military ruler would arise. As the sociologist Max Weber writes: "There was only the intermittent, varying sway of the charismatic war heroes." It was chaotic. Even worse—it relied on the charisma—the great personality—of the individual leader.

While it might be nice to have charismatic leaders, it's hard to rely on them actually turning up when you need them. Charismatic leaders can also be dangerous; think of Hitler and Stalin. Kings become kings not because they are charismatic (in fact, often they are not); they become kings because they "inherit" the job. There are also dangers in having a king: he must not be above the law—he must serve the law. That is why the chapter of the king in Deuteronomy ends by commanding that the king have a copy of Torah right by his side at all times. Now that's a powerful visual aid!

Therefore, why do the people want a king? Because kingship would be far more predictable and stable. Sometimes the right choice is not the perfect choice, but the welfare of the majority is what counts the most.

❖ Notes

❖ Notes

CPSIA information can be obtained
at www.ICGtesting.com
Printed in the USA
LVHW032143171118
597514LV00005BA/395/P